First Edition

ISBN: 978-1-3999-8200-9

# Contents

# No offence intended...

"Speak ~~More~~ Better English," has been written to help us venture together towards mastering the English language, a transformative journey that opens doors to endless possibilities.

I write to you as a young boy, who has had the pleasure of calling both the historic streets of London and the dynamic, tropical city-state of Singapore my home. At the age of 10, I'm eager to share my passion for the English language through this book, which I hope will be a valuable guide for fellow learners.

Singapore, with its towering HDB flats and the aroma of satay perfuming the air at our bustling hawker centres, has cultivated its own brand of English—Singlish. This book, however, aims to complement our local lingo with insights into Standard English, much like how a steaming cup of Milo complements a rainy Singapore afternoon.

The mastery of Standard English can be as invigorating as the feeling of acing the PSLE, opening doors to global dialogues and empowering us with the confidence to navigate diverse academic and professional landscapes. My encounters with friends, both in the shadow of Big Ben and within the verdant parks of Singapore, have highlighted the versatility and value of being adept in the formal variant of English.

In this book, I have identified 30 'problems' found in Singlish and sometimes just informal English. You might choose to dig in once a day keeping you occupied for up to a month.

So, I invite you to join me on this enriching journey. Together, let's explore the realms of Standard English to ensure that we are able to convey clarity across the globe.

# Double negatives

"I don't know nothing! Can you teach me or not?"

# Double negatives

In the sentence, "I don't know nothing! Can you teach me or not?" there is a mistake called a double negative. A double negative occurs when we use two negative words together, which can make the sentence confusing.

In standard English, when we want to say that we don't know anything, we use one negative word. So instead of saying "don't know nothing," we say "don't know anything." The word "nothing" already has a negative meaning, so we don't need to use "don't" with it.

Here's how we can fix the sentence: "I don't know anything! Can you teach me or not?"
By removing one negative word, the sentence becomes clearer and follows the rules of standard English. "I don't know anything" means that you have no knowledge about the topic.

Remember, it's important to use one negative word at a time to avoid confusion. So next time, instead of using "don't know nothing," use "don't know anything" to express that you have no knowledge about something.

# Definitive articles

"I go to library, borrow book"

# Definitive articles

In the sentence, "Go to library lah, borrow book," there is a mistake called missing the definitive article.
In standard English, we use the word "the" before a noun to show that we are talking about a specific thing.

So instead of saying "Go to library," we say "Go to the library." Adding "the" helps us know which library we are talking about.
Here's how we can fix the sentence: "Go to the library lah, borrow a book."

By adding "the" before "library" and using the article "a" before "book," the sentence becomes clearer and follows the rules of standard English.

Remember, when talking about a specific place or thing, we use "the" to help us understand which one we are referring to. So next time, instead of saying "Go to library," say "Go to the library" to indicate a specific library. And don't forget to add "a" before "book" to show that you want to borrow any book.

# Overuse of lah and leh

"Can buy kopi lah? No money, leh."

# Overuse of lah and leh

In Singlish, we often use words like "lah" and "leh" as sentence-ending particles. However, in standard English, these words are not necessary and can make the sentence sound incorrect.

Adding "lah" or "leh" at the end of a sentence doesn't change the meaning, but it's something we use for emphasis or to show our feelings. In standard English, we use different words or expressions to convey those meanings.

For example, instead of saying "I don't want to go, lah!" in standard English, we can say "I really don't want to go."

So, to fix the sentence, we can remove "lah" or "leh" and replace it with suitable words or expressions that express our feelings or emphasize our point.

Remember, it's important to adapt our language to the situation and use appropriate words and expressions in standard English. By doing so, we can communicate clearly and effectively.

# Gender confusion

"My mom went to the store, and he bought groceries."

# Gender confusion

In the sentence, "My mom went to the store, and he bought groceries," there is a mistake called gender confusion. It happens when we use the wrong pronoun to refer to someone's gender.

In this case, "he" is used to refer to "my mom," which can be confusing. To fix it, we need to use the correct pronoun that matches the person's gender.

Here's how we can fix the sentence: "My mom went to the store, and she bought groceries."

By using "she" instead of "he," we make it clear that the pronoun refers to the correct person, which is the mother.

Remember, it's important to use the right pronoun to match someone's gender. So, next time, instead of saying "he" when talking about your mom, use "she" to correctly refer to her.

Understanding and using the correct pronouns helps us communicate clearly and respectfully.

# Tautology

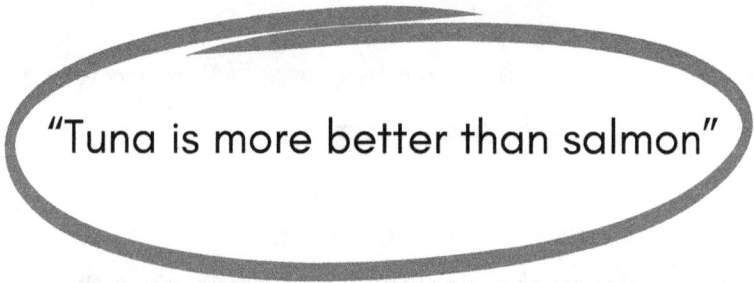

"Tuna is more better than salmon"

# Tautology

In the sentence, "Tuna is more better than salmon," there is a mistake called a comparative error (Tautology). When comparing two things, we use the word "better" instead of "more better."

Here's how we can fix the sentence: "Tuna is better than salmon."
By removing the word "more" and using "better" alone, the sentence becomes correct and follows the rules of standard English.

When we compare two things, we use the word "better" to show that one thing is of higher quality or more suitable than the other. So, next time, instead of saying "more better," use "better" to express that something is superior to something else.

Remember, it's important to use the right words to compare things accurately.

# Tense confusion

"Yesterday, I go to the mall and tomorrow I bought a game"

# Tense confusion

In the sentence, "Yesterday, I go to the mall tomorrow I bought a game" there is a mistake called mixing past, present, and future tense. It's important to use the correct verb tense to show when an action happened.

To fix this, we need to make the verb tenses consistent. Here's how we can do it: "Yesterday, I went to the mall and will buy a new game tomorrow."

In this corrected sentence, we use the past tense "went" to describe the action that happened yesterday, and the future tense "will buy" to talk about the action that will happen tomorrow.

When we talk about something that happened in the past, we use past tense verbs. And when we talk about something that will happen in the future, we use future tense verbs.

Keeping the verb tenses consistent helps us express the sequence of events correctly.

Remember, using the correct verb tense helps us tell stories and share information accurately.

# Redundant tags

"My sister she very tall,"

# Redundant tags

In the sentence, "My sister she very tall," there is a mistake called redundant use of a pronoun. When we mention someone's name or a noun, we don't need to use a pronoun to refer to that person again.

To fix this, we can remove the pronoun "she" and say, "My sister is very tall."

When we say "My sister," the word "sister" already tells us that we are referring to a female person. So, it's not necessary to use the pronoun "she" again.

Pronouns are used to replace nouns and make our sentences shorter and smoother. However, when we explicitly mention the person or noun, we don't need to use the pronoun alongside it.

Remember, when talking about someone, we can use their name or noun directly without adding unnecessary pronouns. By doing this, we can communicate clearly and avoid redundancy in our sentences.

# Singular and plural confusion

"I have 100 cow but 1 cats"

# Singular and plural confusion

In the sentence, "I have 100 cow but 1 cats," there are mistakes related to singular and plural forms. It's important to use the correct form of nouns when talking about quantities.

To fix this, we need to make the nouns agree in number. Here's how we can do it: "I have 100 cows but 1 cat."

In this corrected sentence, we use the plural form "cows" to match the quantity of 100. We also use the singular form "cat" to match the quantity of 1.

When we talk about more than one of something, like cows, we use the plural form. And when we talk about only one of something, like a cat, we use the singular form.

Remember, using the correct singular or plural form helps us express quantities accurately. It's important to match the noun with the correct number.

# Lack of subject verbal agreement

"The boys plays soccer every day."

# Lack of subject verbal agreement

When we say "The boys plays soccer every day.", it is grammatically correct. The word "plays" disagrees with the subject "boys" because "boys" is a plural noun, and we use the singular form of the verb.

To understand this better, let's look at the incorrect sentence as an example: "The boys plays soccer every day." Here, there is a lack of subject-verb agreement.

The verb "plays" is used incorrectly because it is a singular form of the verb, while "boys" is a plural subject.

To fix the mistake, we should say "The boys play soccer every day." This sentence is correct because the verb "play" agrees with the plural subject "boys."

Remember, when the subject is plural, the verb should also be in its plural form. So, next time, say "The boys play soccer every day." to accurately describe the action of multiple boys playing soccer.

# Incomplete comparisons

"This phone is cheaper, faster, and better."

# Incomplete comparisons

In the sentence, "This phone is cheaper, faster, and better," there is a mistake called incomplete comparisons. When we compare things, it's important to provide a clear point of comparison, so that others understand what we are comparing the object to.

To fix this, we need to specify what we are comparing the phone to. Here's an example of a corrected sentence: "This phone is cheaper, faster, and better than the other phone."

In this corrected sentence, we mention "the other phone" as the point of comparison. By doing this, we provide a clear context for the comparisons.

When we compare things, it's important to mention what we are comparing them to, so that our comparisons make sense. We need to specify the object or group of objects we are comparing to show how one thing is better, faster, or cheaper than the other.

Remember, providing complete comparisons helps others understand and appreciate the differences between objects.

**25**

# Incorrect word order

"I can go to the park now?"

# Incorrect word order

In the sentence, "I can go the park now?" there is a mistake in word order. When asking a question in English, we need to follow a specific word order to make it clear and understandable.

To fix this, we need to rearrange the words. Here's an example of a corrected sentence: "Can I go to the park now?"

In this corrected sentence, we start with the helping verb "Can" to form a question. Then we use the subject pronoun "I" to refer to ourselves. Next, we include the verb "go" to show the action of going, followed by the preposition "to" to indicate the destination, which in this case is "the park."

When asking questions in English, we typically start with a helping verb, then include the subject, followed by the main verb and any necessary words to complete the sentence.

Remember, using the correct word order helps us ask questions in a clear and understandable way.

# Incorrect use of adverbs

"I can't, very tired run fast."

# Incorrect use of adverbs

In the sentence, "I can't, very tired run fast," there is a mistake in the use of the adverb "very." Adverbs are used to describe or modify verbs, adjectives, or other adverbs. However, in this sentence, "very" is used incorrectly before the verb "tired."

To fix this, we need to use the adverb "very" in the correct context. Here's an example of a corrected sentence: "I am very tired. I can't run fast."

In this corrected sentence, we start with the phrase "I am" to indicate the state of being. Then we use the adverb "very" to modify the adjective "tired," expressing a strong degree of tiredness. Finally, we state the consequence of being tired by saying "I can't run fast."

When using adverbs, it's important to place them appropriately to modify the right part of the sentence. In this case, "very" should be used to describe how tired we are, not the action of running.

Remember, using adverbs correctly helps us express ourselves more accurately.

# Pronoun disagreement

"She go to the park."

# Pronoun disagreement

In the sentence, "She go to the park," there is a mistake called pronoun disagreement. Pronouns are words we use to replace nouns, like "she" instead of saying someone's name. When we use a pronoun, we need to make sure it matches the verb form.

To fix this, we need to use the correct verb form that matches the pronoun "she." Here's an example of a corrected sentence: "She goes to the park."

In this corrected sentence, we use the verb form "goes" to match the singular subject pronoun "she." When we talk about someone doing an action in the present, we add an "s" to the verb form after the pronoun "she."

It's important to use the correct verb form that matches the subject of the sentence. When talking about someone else, like "she," we need to change the verb form to show agreement.

Remember, using the right verb form helps us communicate accurately. So, instead of saying "She go to the park," use "She goes to the park" to show that she is the one doing the action.

**31**

# Incorrect subject-verb agreement

"I'm going to the market at Orchard Road."

# Incorrect subject-verb agreement

In the sentence, "I'm going to the market at Orchard Road," there is a mistake in the choice of preposition. Prepositions are words we use to show relationships between objects, people, or places. In this case, the preposition "at" is used incorrectly.

To fix this, we need to use the correct preposition that matches the situation. Here's an example of a corrected sentence: "I'm going to the market in Orchard Road."

In this corrected sentence, we use the preposition "in" to indicate that the market is located within Orchard Road. When we want to show that something is inside a particular place, like a road, we use the preposition "in" instead of "at."

It's important to choose the right preposition to accurately describe the location. So, instead of saying "at Orchard Road," we say "in Orchard Road" to show that the market is within the road.

Remember, using the correct preposition helps us communicate more accurately.

# Incomplete sentences

"Going school late."

# Incomplete sentences

In the sentence, "Going school late," there is a mistake called an incomplete sentence.

Sentences in English typically need a subject (who or what the sentence is about) and a verb (the action or state of being). In this case, the sentence is missing both.

To fix this, we need to include the subject and verb to make a complete sentence. Here's an example of a corrected sentence: "I am going to school late."

In this corrected sentence, we start with the subject pronoun "I" to indicate who is performing the action. Then we include the verb "am" to show the present tense of the verb "going." Finally, we add the preposition "to" before the noun "school" to indicate the destination.

When constructing sentences, it's important to include both a subject and a verb to convey a complete thought. In this case, instead of saying "Going school late," we say "I am going to school late" to provide clarity and make the sentence grammatically correct.

Remember, using complete sentences helps us express ourselves clearly.

# Misplacing apostrophes

"That's it's color!"

# Misplacing apostrophes

In the sentence, "That's it's color!" there is a mistake called misplacing the apostrophe. An apostrophe is a punctuation mark used to show possession or to indicate a contraction (combining two words).

In this case, the word "it's" is used incorrectly. "It's" is a contraction of "it is" and not used to show possession. Instead, we should use "its" without an apostrophe to indicate possession.

To fix the sentence, we can say, "That's its color!"
In this corrected sentence, we remove the apostrophe from "it's" and use "its" to indicate that the color belongs to something. "Its" is used to show possession when something belongs to "it."

Remember, when using "its," there is no need for an apostrophe. The word "it's" with an apostrophe is used to mean "it is." So, instead of saying "That's it's color!", we say "That's its color!" to show that the color belongs to something.

# Incorrect comparative form

"This is the goodest cake I've
ever tasted!"

# Incorrect comparative form

In the sentence, "This is the goodest cake I've ever tasted!" there is a mistake in using the comparative form of the word "good."

When we compare two things, we use the word "better" instead of "goodest."

To fix this, we should use the word "best" instead of "goodest." Here's an example of a corrected sentence: "This is the best cake I've ever tasted!"

In this corrected sentence, we use the word "best" to indicate the highest level of quality or excellence. When something is better than all the others, we use "best" as the superlative form of "good."

Remember, when comparing two things, we use "better," and when we want to say something is the highest or topmost, we use "best." So instead of saying "This is the goodest cake," we say "This is the best cake" to express that it is of the highest quality.

By using the correct comparative and superlative forms, you can improve your English skills and communicate more accurately!

# Confusing "fewer" and "less"

"I have less books than him."

# Confusing "fewer" and "less"

In the sentence, "I have less books than him," there is a mistake in using the words "less" and "fewer." These words are used to compare quantities, but they have different usage rules.

To fix this, we should use the word "fewer" instead of "less." Here's an example of a corrected sentence: "I have fewer books than him."

In this corrected sentence, we use "fewer" to indicate a smaller number of countable items, like books. When we can count the items individually, we use "fewer" to compare quantities.

The word "less" is used when we cannot count the items individually, like sand or water. For example, we say "I have less water" because water is not something we can count.

So instead of saying "I have less books," we say "I have fewer books" to indicate that the number of books is smaller in comparison.

Remember, when comparing countable items, use "fewer," and when comparing uncountable items, use "less." By using these words correctly, you can improve your English skills and communicate more accurately!

# Misusing articles

"I have an cat."

# Misusing articles

In the sentence, "I have an cat," there is a mistake in using the article "an." Articles are small words used before nouns to indicate whether we are talking about a specific or non-specific thing.

To fix this, we should use the article "a" instead of "an." Here's an example of a corrected sentence: "I have a cat."

In this corrected sentence, we use "a" before the word "cat" because "cat" starts with a consonant sound. When we talk about something in general, we use "a" before countable nouns that start with consonant sounds.

The article "an" is used before words that start with vowel sounds. For example, we say "an apple" because "apple" starts with a vowel sound.

So instead of saying "I have an cat," we say "I have a cat" to indicate that we own a cat.

Remember, if a noun starts with a consonant sound, use "a," and if it starts with a vowel sound, use "an." By using the correct article, you can improve your English skills!

# Overusing filler words

"Um, like, you know, I mean, I was, like, going to the store"

# Overusing filler words

In the sentence, "Um, like, you know, I mean, I was, like, going to the store," there are several filler words used excessively. Filler words are words or phrases that are used to pause or fill gaps in speech, but when overused, they can make your speech less clear and effective.

Using excessive filler words can make it difficult for others to understand your message and can distract from what you are trying to say. It's essential to minimize their use to communicate more clearly.

To fix this, try using fewer filler words and speak more directly. Here's an example of a corrected sentence: "I was going to the store."

In this corrected sentence, we remove the unnecessary filler words ("Um, like, you know, I mean") to make the sentence more concise and clear. By eliminating these fillers, your message will be more focused and easier to understand.

Remember, it's important to speak clearly and directly to convey your thoughts effectively. Minimizing the use of filler words will help you communicate more confidently and ensure that your message is heard.

# Using the wrong words

"I'm so exciting lah!"

# Using the wrong words

When we say "I'm so exciting lah!" we are making a mistake in English grammar.

The word "exciting" is an adjective that describes something that makes us feel excited. However, when we talk about how we feel, we should use the adjective "excited" instead of "exciting."

To fix the mistake, we should say "I'm so excited lah!" The word "excited" describes how we feel, and it is the right word to use when talking about our emotions.

Let's understand this with an example: Imagine you're going to a fun amusement park. You can say, "I'm so excited lah!" This means you feel really happy and thrilled about going to the amusement park.

Remember, when talking about your feelings, it's important to use the correct words. Instead of saying "exciting," use "excited" to describe how you feel.

So, next time, remember to say, "I'm so excited lah!" when you're really looking forward to something fun.

# Using incorrect verb forms

"I seen that movie already,"

# Using incorrect verb forms

When we say "I seen that movie already," we are making a mistake in English grammar. The word "seen" is the past participle form of the verb "see," but when we talk about something that happened in the past and is still connected to the present, we should use the present perfect tense.

To fix the mistake, we should say "I have seen that movie already." The words "have seen" tell us that the action of watching the movie happened in the past, but it's important to mention that it is connected to the present.

Let's understand this with an example: Imagine you're talking to your friend about a movie you watched. Instead of saying "I seen that movie already," you should say, "I have seen that movie already." This means that you watched it in the past, but it's still relevant to the present conversation.

Remember, when talking about things that happened in the past but are still important now, we use the present perfect tense. So, next time, say "I have seen" instead of "I seen" to express that you watched something in the past.

# Misusing reflexive pronouns

"He gave the present to myself, lah!"

# Misusing reflexive pronouns

When we say "He gave the present to myself," we are making a mistake in English grammar.

The word "myself" is a reflexive pronoun, which means it is used when the subject of the sentence is also the object of the action.

However, in this sentence, "myself" is not needed because "me" is the correct pronoun to use when someone gives us something.

To fix the mistake, we should say "He gave the present to me, lah!" The word "me" is the correct pronoun to use when we talk about receiving something from someone.

Let's understand this with an example: Imagine your friend gave you a gift. Instead of saying "He gave the present to myself," you should say, "He gave the present to me, lah!" This means that your friend gave the gift directly to you.

Remember, when someone gives you something, use the pronoun "me" to talk about receiving it. So, next time, say "He gave the present to me" instead of "myself" to express that someone gave you something.

**51**

# Misusing prepositions

"I'm excited about go on holiday, lah!"

# Misusing prepositions

When we say "I'm excited about go on holiday," we are making a mistake in English grammar.

In this sentence, we need to use the base form of the verb "go" instead of the word "go" itself. To talk about an action or activity that we are excited about, we should use the -ing form of the verb.

To fix the mistake, we should say "I'm excited about going on holiday, lah!" The word "going" is the -ing form of the verb "go" and is used to express an action or activity that we are excited about.

Let's understand this with an example: Imagine you're eagerly looking forward to your upcoming holiday. Instead of saying "I'm excited about go on holiday," you should say, "I'm excited about going on holiday, lah!" This means that you're thrilled and can't wait for the holiday to happen.

Remember, when talking about an action or activity that you're excited about, use the -ing form of the verb. So, next time, say "I'm excited about going" instead of "go" to express your enthusiasm for something.

# Incorrect use of possessive pronouns

"The book is mines!"

# Incorrect use of possessive pronouns

When we say "The book is mines," we are making a mistake in English grammar. Instead of using the word "mines," we should use the word "mine" to show possession. "Mine" is a possessive pronoun that indicates ownership.

To fix the mistake, we should say "The book is mine, lah!" The word "mine" tells us that the book belongs to us.

Let's understand this with an example: Imagine you're talking about a book that you own.

Instead of saying "The book is mines," you should say, "The book is mine!" This means that the book belongs to you.

Remember, when talking about something that belongs to you, use the word "mine" instead of "mines." So, next time, say "The book is mine" to show that you own it.

# Confusing "then" and "than"

"He is taller then me,"

# Confusing "then" and "than"

When we say "He is taller then me," we are making a mistake in English grammar.

The word "then" is used to indicate a sequence of events or time. However, in this context, we need to use the word "than" to make a comparison between two things or people.

To fix the mistake, we should say "He is taller than me." The word "than" is used to compare the height between two people.

Let's understand this with an example: Imagine you're comparing your height with your friend. Instead of saying

"He is taller then me," you should say, "He is taller than me." This means that your friend has a greater height than you.

Remember, when comparing two things or people, use the word "than" instead of "then." So, next time, say "taller than" to make a comparison between heights.

# Mispronouncing words

"I like ice cream, ekspecialy mint flavour"

# Mispronouncing words

When we say "I like ice cream, ekspecialy mint flavour," we are making a few mistakes in English grammar. The word "ekspecialy" is spelled incorrectly, and the word "flavour" is spelled in the British English way. Additionally, the word "especially" is used incorrectly in the sentence.

To fix the mistakes, we should say "I like ice cream, especially mint flavor." The word "especially" is used to highlight something specific or give emphasis, and "flavor" is the correct spelling in American English.

Let's understand this with an example: Imagine you're talking about your favorite ice cream. Instead of saying "I like ice cream, ekspecialy mint flavour," you should say, "I like ice cream, especially mint flavor." This means that you enjoy ice cream, with a special liking for the mint flavor.

Remember, use the word "especially" to show emphasis and "flavor" (or "flavour" in British English) to talk about different tastes. So, next time, say "especially mint flavor" to express your preference.

# Confusing "hear" and "here"

"I can't here what you're saying, lah!"

# Confusing "hear" and "here"

When we say "I can't here what you're saying, lah!" we are making a mistake in English grammar. The word "here" is used incorrectly in this context. Instead, we should use the word "hear" to indicate the ability to perceive sounds.

To fix the mistake, we should say "I can't hear what you're saying, lah!" The word "hear" means to listen and understand the sounds around you.

Let's understand this with an example: Imagine you're having a conversation with your friend, but you're having trouble understanding them.

Instead of saying "I can't here what you're saying, lah!" you should say, "I can't hear what you're saying, lah!" This means that you're having difficulty perceiving or understanding the words your friend is speaking.

Remember, when you're unable to understand someone's words, use the word "hear" instead of "here." So, next time, say "I can't hear what you're saying, lah!" to express that you're having trouble understanding someone's words.

**61**

# Misusing adverbs and adjectives

"He did good on the test,"

# Misusing adverbs and adjectives

When we say "He did good on the test, lah!" we are making a mistake in English grammar. The word "good" is used incorrectly in this context. Instead, we should use the word "well" to describe how someone performed on a test.

To fix the mistake, we should say "He did well on the test, lah!" The word "well" means to perform in a satisfactory or successful manner.

Let's understand this with an example: Imagine your friend asks you about someone's performance on a test.

Instead of saying "He did good on the test, lah!" you should say, "He did well on the test, lah!" This means that the person performed satisfactorily or successfully on the test.

Remember, when describing someone's performance, use the word "well" instead of "good." So, next time, say "He did well on the test," to express that someone performed successfully on a test.

# Confusing "your" and "you're"

"You're bag is nice!"

# Confusing "your" and "you're"

When we say "You're bag is nice!" we are making a mistake in English grammar. The word "you're" is used incorrectly in this context. Instead, we should use the word "your" to indicate it isn't "you are."

To fix the mistake, we should say "Your bag is nice!" The word "you're" is a contraction of "you are" and is used to describe something about a person.

Let's understand this with an example: Imagine you're complimenting your friend's bag. Instead of saying "You're bag is nice!" you should say, "Your bag is nice!"

This means that the bag belongs to your friend, and you're expressing that it looks good or attractive.

Remember, when talking about someone's possession, use "your" instead of "you're." So, next time, say "Your bag is nice!" to compliment someone's bag.

9 781399 982009